I WAS SET UP TO BE
BLESSED

BY

LAKISHA WILLIAMS

May you experience the blessings
of Ezekiel 34:26 in every are
of your life.

LAKISHA WILLIAMS

TABLE OF CONTENTS

PREFACE

This book is about hope, encouragement, and my journey in life. It's for everyone going through the storm of life or stuck in any area of their life. This book is ... Hope for the hopeless!

ACKNOWLEDGMENT

I would like to acknowledge my hero, my mother of blessed memory, Mrs. Constancia, AKA Mamasita, for her love for me, the wisdom she imparted onto me, and the very many lessons of life she taught me are quite invaluable. She was the strongest person I ever knew. Losing her to death was highly devastating, but God was there to comfort me, and it has been sufficient for me thus far. This session will be futile if I fail to acknowledge my aunts for being there for me when I needed them the most and still being there for me even as we speak; I am very grateful to you all! To my good friends who have been there for me through thick and thin, I want you to know that I do not take this for granted and will forever appreciate you all for all the sacrifices. I may not have a lot of friends, but I will always be grateful to God for the few good ones I have in my life. To my friend, Whitney, who introduced me to her Pastor, Prophetess Denise, who is now my pastor, too, I say a big thank you. Prophetess Denise has been a blessing ever since I joined the ministry. Very importantly, I would like to thank all those who kept asking me when I would write a book; you all spurred me on to these great feet I have attained today. The book is finally here for you! Above all, my sincere appreciation goes to the almighty God for His endless blessings in my life and for the inspiration and wisdom to write this book. The joy of today's success and history as an author in my life couldn't have been without you!

DEDICATION

I dedicate this book to everyone who asks me for advice, reads my message on Facebook, Instagram, or Twitter; this book was written with you in mind, and I hope it will remind you that you can bounce back from everything. I hope this book will encourage you to go after your dreams, no matter how big they are, because it's good if the dream scares you, implying you need God's help to accomplish it and you can do all things through Christ who strengthens you. I also want to dedicate this book to everyone out there suffering from self-doubt. Stop now! Just do it like Nike! You only fail when you don't try!

CHAPTER 1

PEACE IN THE MIDST OF LIFE STORMS

"Worry about nothing. Pray about everything"- Philippians 4:6

When my mother passed on to be with the Lord, it brought a lot of uncertainty. I was unsure about many things, which caused me to worry about everything. When my mother was sick, I trusted God to heal her, but that never happened, as He eventually called her home to Himself. Even though my human nature would want to ask God why He had to call her to himself by this time, I had to trust God and know that all things would work out for my good, be it good, bad, ugly, or uncomfortable.

I do worry these days, but I do more praying than worrying, which soothes my soul and causes me to sleep at night. Knowing that God knows my present and future brings me comfort. Worrying makes no sense. It's an unnecessary and needless act we're all guilty of because a critical look at it will show you that you eventually got or got over, today, the things you worried about yesterday. Worrying has never solved a situation before. If God has not willed it, no amount of worrying can bring any result for you, even if you add action pans to it. So, cast all your worries on God, as He has promised to always come through for us.

After my older brother was deported to Panama, I worried about him and the family he left behind here in America. I worried if he would attend my wedding or other important events in my life, but our thoughts are not His thoughts, neither are our ways His ways. His children are older now, and they go to Panama as a family to visit him. Though this might not be the best family experience they crave, but, as I said before, God works all things out for our good. He is still in communication with his children, and they visit him, and I believe that someday they will all reunite, in Jesus' name, amen. That's why there is no need to worry; God always has a way out for us, no matter the circumstance or situation. As for my wedding, if need be, I will have a destination wedding. When the time is right, the decision will be made. This is why there is no need to worry.

Since my mother passed three years ago, I have lived with my dad. He has a little issue with his leg that has left him at the mercy of a walking stick, making me stick around without thinking of moving cities or countries out of worry for how he will cope all by himself. However, the reality is that God will heal him, and he will be ok; all I have to do is trust Him. God is ready to get me started with my life now with the many doors he has opened for me; He is ready to grant me my own place, and my dad's issue is not severe. He can take care of himself, and I won't move too far; I will only be about 30 minutes away. I presently reside in the Bronx, but my heart is in Brooklyn. I love Brooklyn, like cooked food! My father has given me his blessing, which is another reason I don't have to worry. More importantly, God has given me the pass to go.

Worrying is unhealthy for you. It causes frustration, high blood pressure, sleepless nights, stress, hair loss, and inability to think or function properly. So, the best thing to do is take it to God in prayer and wait for instructions because He knows what tomorrow holds. God knows your future; therefore, it's better to talk to Him about your plans to see if they align with His. The Scripture says in Proverbs 16:9 (NLT), *"We can make our plans, but the Lord determines our steps."* This is why you have to ensure that what you want to do is what God wants you to do to avoid wasting time and resources. Always remember that when God gives you something, it does not burden or bring you sorrow. So, if what you are stepping into is stressing you out or causing you sleepless nights, it's not from God. Always ensure you take it to God in prayer and wait for direction as to what step you should take or do a whole new thing.

A lot of the things we take the time to worry about in our lives, we eventually experience but are not hurt. In fact, they have helped us get to the next place God wants us to be. This is why it doesn't make sense to worry about things. For example, I worried about what would happen to my family when my older brother got deported, and I can tell you that we are good. It all worked out. At the time, I worried about it, but God worked it out as I worried. It all worked out. It may not have been how I wanted it to work out, but it was still good. As against my fears, things didn't destroy. This is why it's a total waste of time to worry because, eventually, things will work out for your good. Our human nature, at times, doesn't allow us to trust that God will work it out. However, as we mature and see God come through for us, time and time again, It helps build our faith and believe that next time we won't need to worry about it because the same God that came through for us will come through for us again.

Often, we don't do something because we worry about what others would think or say. But at the end of the day, they don't matter. Many won't understand what was put in you, and that's ok. Your fingerprint does not match anyone else's fingerprint, so you cannot expect people to like or agree with everything you do or say. There is an audience for everybody — what one person does not like, another will. The people you are supposed to reach with your content will wholly accept you. Those that don't, simply don't matter, and

I say this in the most respectful way. They don't matter because it wasn't meant for them. Those that received it with open arms are the ones it was meant for; they are the ones that will receive it and run with it.

"Write down, 10 different things that are bothering you right now, after reading this chapter."

_____

_____

_____

_____

_____

_____

_____

_____

_____

_____

_____

_____

_____

_____

_____

_____

_____

"Write down 10 things that you are grateful for after, reading this chapter."

_____

_____

_____

_____

_____

_____

_____

_____

_____

_____

_____

_____

_____

_____

_____

_____

CHAPTER 2

NEVER DESPISE SMALL BEGINNINGS

Zechariah 4:10

U nderstand that your current situation is not your final destination. It doesn't matter what you may be facing now; it's temporal; glory days await after this. Your struggles wouldn't last forever; they are just seasons you must go through before you experience the promised land—the land of milk and honey. You must go through those trying times before you can worthily eat the good of the land. You're made to go through those moments so you can appreciate the blessings that come after! Things cannot just be handed to you because you won't appreciate them. So, understand that it won't always be like this. God sends rain on the just as well as to the unjust.

When I was in junior high school, my mother never wanted me to work, but I would go to the supermarket with my cousins and pack bags. I used to make money packing bags and making deliveries. Packing bags taught me to work for my money. Fast-forward to now, I'm established with a master's degree. So, never despise small beginnings. Everything you go through in life shapes you and makes you into what you are today. One thing about God, He wastes nothing. Packing bags taught me to hustle. That's why today I stand as an entrepreneur with three businesses. I am a hustler, a trait that developed in me from a young age. It is something I carried with me into my adulthood. God gives us the power to gain wealth. He downloads ideas and strategies to you that will cause you to prosper. His Word says so! See Deuteronomy 8:18 (KJV), *"but thou shalt remember the Lord thy God: for it is He that giveth thee power to get wealth, that He may establish His covenant which He sware unto thy fathers, as it is this day."*

I remember asking myself why certain people had more than me when I was younger. I am a good person. I failed to understand then that it's not about being a good person; when it's your turn, it's your turn. That was my small beginning. That was the young me. I look at all I have today at my age and can never ask why someone else is blessed than I am because the gift of life alone is enough to give God praise. I have so much stuff that I can give ten or more bags away and still have a lot left. Where you are today is not where you will be one year or one month from now. So, it is always good to ask God what He wants you to learn from your current state because He wastes nothing, and everything is for a purpose.

If you pay attention to the stories of many millionaires and Billionaires, you will realize that most of them didn't start out with a lot — it was accumulated. Many of them were homeless and looked down on, but understand that after you hit rock bottom, the only other place to go is up. When you don't have much growing up, it is a different kind of hunger. It drives you to reach for the stars and never end up at that low place ever again in your life. It stretches you; it motivates you. It teaches you humility and causes you to never look down on anyone or compare yourself to anyone because you don't know people's life stories. You only see them at their glory, totally ignorant of what they had to endure to reach their place of abundance.

With God on your side, even your worst day will be your best day because joy comes in the morning. God hears the cries of His people. What you may be experiencing right now is just for a while; nothing lasts forever. You have to understand that it is not forever, and it is here to teach you something. Get the lesson and move on. If you don't, you will repeat the course until the lesson is learned. Don't be like the Israelites and go around the same mountain for forty years when the journey was just supposed to be for eleven days. They ended up dying there because they complained and murmured. Get the lesson and move on because a great future lies before you if you can just get through your current situation. You are stronger than you think you are.

Let's examine a butterfly. It doesn't start off as a butterfly. It takes time. It starts off as an egg, then a caterpillar, and finally becomes a butterfly. Before this transformation, you will see an egg and not think it will become such a beautiful butterfly. It is the same thing with our lives. Where you are, presently, is not where you will end up. This is just the beginning. You are being shaped and molded into the best you can be. All you have to do is keep striving, stay consistent, and eventually, you will be the person you are supposed to be. Things often start off bad, but that does not mean we will remain there forever. That's just one chapter of your life; there are more chapters left to be written. It is only over when you give up. So, stay the course and keep going. There is more for you if you can believe it.

If you are still alive and have breath in your body, God is not finished with you. That means there is still hope for you to shake yourself out of any situation and keep on striving for greatness. Just because you failed a few times and made mistakes doesn't mean it's over. It only shows you are human. It is ok to fail at things; let no one tell you otherwise. You have to keep trying until something works for you. Always remember that you are only a failure when you stop trying. So, keep pushing, keep striving, and keep hoping because it will all make sense one day. It will work out one day, as long as you keep trying and never give up.

"Write down, 10 different things that are bothering you right now, after reading this chapter."

_____

_____

_____

_____

_____

_____

_____

_____

_____

_____

_____

_____

_____

_____

_____

"Write down 10 things that you are grateful for after, reading this chapter."

_____

_____

_____

_____

_____

_____

_____

_____

_____

_____

_____

_____

_____

_____

_____

_____

CHAPTER 3

YOU WERE SEPARATED TO BE ELEVATED

God has a purpose for each and every one of us. However, you may not have tapped into it just yet. Some people discover their purpose as they go through the different trials of life, which is why it's good to seek God's face in getting out of this situation. It's worthy of note that it's not good to complain because when you do, you remain where you are, but when you praise, you will be raised. Praising God will get your mind off your problems. It will also confuse the enemy.

If you look back over your life, you will see the times God hid you from people. He strategically removed people from your life for you to grow and trust Him. There are people in our life that mean evil for us. They are there to use and abuse us. Sometimes, we fail to recognize who we are, so we stick around until strong enough to leave. There are friends you were once very close to until God gradually removed them from your life. Why? Because they did not have your best interest at heart, they can't go where God is taking you, and more importantly, they were never your friend. They were your enemy the whole time.

I had this female friend; we were super cool. I used to stay at her house, and we did everything together. After high school, she got pregnant, married, and had two kids while I chose to continue my education. We kept in contact, and I visited her in Brooklyn all the time. After I began prospering, things changed. She never applauded or cheered for me; instead, it seemed as though she enjoyed seeing me fail and in pain. I blocked her from everything; I don't wish her any harm, though. She was never my friend; she was just a hater disguised as a friend and was only ok when I was doing ok; the moment I surpassed her, it became a problem. You need to recognize that those kinds of people have got to go; they have no business being around you. Some people see what you have inside of you and try to destroy it, which is why it's good to know who you are and whose you are. You are royalty. Never forget that.

We can look at the story of Joseph in the Bible. He was separated to be elevated, according to Genesis 37-50. His brothers betrayed him, and consequently, he went through a lot and ultimately ended up being second in command of Egypt. Then God caused a famine in the land. This famine caused his brothers to come to Egypt for food. Joseph could have gotten revenge on his brothers, but he didn't. He was motivated by love. He helped them instead. This story teaches us that what others meant for evil; God turns it all around for our good.

When you are separated from certain people, your life begins to flourish. This is because they were no good for you. They hinder your progress. Some people stay around you to mess up everything you good you decide to embark on. They are dream killers — you tell them your dreams and goals, and they pray it never happens for you. Some people are so evil they will say things like over their dead body will you get married, prosper, own a house or buy a car. Some people are wicked, and this is why you must detach yourself from them as soon as possible. You may have them in your life now, undetected, but to fish them out, just listen to the things that people say to you when you come to them with good news or ideas. They will tell you how they really feel, and if you're attentive enough, you will hear or see it in their response and countenance.

Some people ask me why I am always alone. The truth is I enjoy being alone. It brings less problems. I would rather be alone than with a bad company because such a company corrupts good character. I don't trust a lot of people, so consequently, I am always all by myself a lot of the time. I have a few good friends, which is good enough for me. Understand that it is quality over quantity. The only thing you need a lot of it is money, but you actually need to have wisdom and know-how to manage the money.

We often wait for our time to come, but it doesn't come when we desire because of the kind of company we keep. Some of those around us are dreams and vision killers. Watch those friends who tell you things like, "you can't do that", "that is beyond you", "that is too big for you to do". What those friends do is project their fear and inability on you. Just because they cannot do it does not mean you can't do it. You are different. You trust and believe God. He is inside of you, and there is nothing you cannot do. This is why you don't have to share your big dreams with just anybody. People will get jealous of you because of your dream. That's exactly what Joseph's brothers did to him; they threw him in a pit because his dream was too big. This is why a separation has to take place. God cannot give you certain things or take you to certain places until you get rid of those parasitic people around you. All they do is to leech you.

Know those around you so that you can see where the discrepancy is taking place. Some people only come to take from you. Those people need no access to your life. Some people, when they come into your life, it turns sour — everything goes bad until they leave. When you cut certain people from your space, you will see things begin to flow in your life. Some people are born haters, and because they cannot accomplish certain things, they will try to stop you from accomplishing yours. Recognize those people and don't allow them access to you again.

"Write down, 10 different things that are bothering you right now, after reading this chapter."

_____

_____

_____

_____

_____

_____

_____

_____

_____

_____

_____

_____

_____

_____

_____

_____

_____

_____

"Write down 10 things that you are grateful for after, reading this chapter."

_____

_____

_____

_____

_____

_____

_____

_____

_____

_____

_____

_____

_____

_____

_____

_____

_____

_____

CHAPTER 4

IT IS NEVER TOO LATE TO BEGIN AGAIN

Y ou can be so foolish at times when you are young, but that's ok. You can dust yourself off and start again. Once you make up your mind never to remain in the same place again, the sky will be your limit from there. Time and time again, I have watched people bounce back from bad situations. It can be hard sometimes, but you have to seek God to help you, and in doing that, He will show you who you really are and strengthen you along the way.

I remember in 2017 when I left the department of corrections because I gave an inmate my phone number. Strange, right? Yeah, up to this date, I still don't even know why I did it, too. Like, what was I thinking? I messed up big time, but God showed me mercy for my ignorance and opened the door of another job for me somewhere else once I stopped having a pity party. Many people came up to me and said, "How could you mess up a job where you can earn $100,000 or more?" I don't know. I guess it wasn't meant for me to be there, that's why. Most people do things for the money, and my heart wasn't in being a correctional officer any way because I hated it over time. I love to hang out. So, I resigned to be able to work for the City. God then opened another door for me. I thank God for my mom because she gave me a soft landing and never worsened my already messed up state with harsh reception and words. She was like, "I didn't want you to work there, anyway". A lot of my friends and family members felt the same. So, I moved on peacefully. Everyone else who thought and felt otherwise didn't matter.

God was truly on my side. I started working at the Gap on 42nd street, and within a week, I got a promotion. Then a friend told me about a case manager job. I was able to secure that and subsequently reenrolled into John Jay to finish my master's degree. Accidentally, I went to class thinking I had to make a presentation for my paper but later realized I didn't have to when the professor informed me otherwise. However, while in the class, someone gave a presentation and talked about the company they work for. After they were done, I asked if they were hiring. They said yes, so I sent in my resume on Friday, and they called me by Monday. God had his hand on me all the while. Mind you; I wasn't able to find the classroom at first. The enemy was trying to keep me from this opportunity, but God never allowed it!

There are instances where you think you cannot come back from a situation, but you definitely can. I know people who got deported to their country of origin and haven't been back since their youth but are free and making it over there. It is never too late to begin again. I remember being in ridiculous relationships with individuals who had two baby mommas. One told me that a girl had rapped him, while another accidentally showed me the picture of a female in front of his TV that wasn't his mother, sister, or cousin. These kinds of relationships remind you that you can definitely do better. God hides your worth from people because He doesn't want you with them. God will cause everything to go wrong in the relationship because He doesn't want you there. That's why I noticed that most of my relationships were the same, just different men. The reason for this was that I didn't learn my lesson. I was too good for them and was settling for less when God had so much more for me. As I began to mature and realize my true worth, I did notice that I didn't stay in relationships as long as I used to. It would last two to three months or less if they were not consistent.

I see where I am and where I came from, and I give God praise for it all. Some people are not worth your peace, joy, time, or happiness. This goes for family, friends, and relationships. Learn to love yourself and trust God to make all things work out for your good. Understand that you only see people's faces but not the intentions of their hearts. So, you have to exercise wisdom and ask God to grant you discernment because there are lots of wolves in sheep clothing in these streets waiting for an opportunity to get you off track. Some people will come into your life to do that; they are there to derail you. The enemy also knows what you like, so he can send a man or woman to you carry out this work of destruction in your life — someone that will cause you to lose everything. Then after you leave them and are no longer associated with them, you see

31

your life heading in the direction it was meant to go all along. Why? Because they were destiny killers. The enemy assigned them to get you off track. Keep your eyes open.

The enemy does not have any new tricks up his sleeves — don't be fooled. When people come into your life, take them to God in prayer before bringing them close to you. Don't take people at face value. Some are just there to stop you from doing well. They will pretend to be on your side when, in reality, they are poking holes in your boat to sink and destroy you. You may be wondering why you feel like you are drowning; you may also feel like things are going wrong all of a sudden; the reason for this is not farfetched. It's because of what you have allowed in your space. Some people bring bad energy and vibe with them. That is why you can be around certain people and don't feel right. This is because some people carry heavy spirits with them, hence the need to test the spirit. Once you have checked people out with God, you can proceed to entertain them. Some people are not worth your time or energy. So, check them out to avoid any heart or headache.

"Write down, 10 different things that are bothering you right now, after reading this chapter."

_____

_____

_____

_____

_____

_____

_____

_____

_____

_____

_____

_____

_____

_____

_____

_____

_____

_____

_____

"Write down 10 things that you are grateful for after, reading this chapter."

CHAPTER 5

IF YOU AIM AT NOTHING, YOU WILL HIT IT EVERY TIME

What are your goals? What are your aspirations? Make a list and check it twice. If you are not aiming for anything, you will remain in the same place. The devil cannot stand a moving target. He attacks you the most when you are stagnant and isolated. Keep it moving! You cannot be in the same place you were last month. There has to be some time of change in your life. A bill you paid off, a pound or two you lost. There has to be something you accomplish daily, weekly, monthly, or yearly.

When the pandemic hit, a lot of people became entrepreneurs. What were you doing? There has to be something you desire more than lying in your bed at night, drinking, smoking weed, etc. Take a look at your life; if you don't like certain things, change them. Work on your credit, pay your bills off, buy a house, buy a car, go on vacation, and buy some stocks. Do something. Set some goals. Go on a weight loss journey, write a book. Set some goals and stick to them because I would rather ask for something big and get some of it than ask for something small and get all of it. Aim big!

Surround yourself with people that are going places. Examine the people around you. Most of the time, you are where you are due to the company you keep. Surround yourself with people that can pull you up and who you can learn something from. If you are the smartest one in the group, then you need a new group. Always have people around you that you strive to be like; do not hate. Take notes so you can go to the next level. Always have people around you that you look up to so you don't remain in the same place. Life is about growing and going from level to level. Make sure you are reaching and aiming for better and not worst.

It is time to stop going around the same mountain. Your life should not be like a roller coaster. One day you're up, and another day you're down. That is not God's will for your life. This is why it is good to look at your life and figure out what produces fruit and what doesn't. If someone is constantly taking and draining you, they need to go. If it is not adding to your life, subtract it from your life. Simple as that. Make sure everything in your life is bearing fruit because if it's not, it's a hindrance, and it is stopping you from making the necessary moves that will bring you closer to your destiny.

As you aim toward what you want and what you feel you deserve, what you used to like wouldn't taste the same anymore. The taste in men changes along with other things. That's called maturity. This is when you know you are growing and pressing toward bigger and better things. Always have goals so as not to be stagnant. Understand that you can do all things with Christ who strengthens you, so take the limits off. Just because they cannot do it does not mean you cannot do it. God lives in you, and there is no limit for God. So, aim so high that it surprises you and blows your mind because that is what God has called us to do, great exploits. With God by your side, you are the majority and can do mighty things.

People never want you to arrive at a destination they haven't been to themself. You are not them, and you should never allow anyone to stop you from surpassing them. A lot of people start and do not finish. Many get lazy along the way. Some get distracted, and many procrastinate. But you have to make up in your mind that whatever you start, you have to finish. The Bible says that better is the end of a thing than the beginning. So, you can start all you want, but if you don't finish, it is better you didn't start at all. If you don't finish what you start, you won't be able to reap the benefits of the fruit of your labor.

To avoid aiming at something and not hitting the target, never take on more than you can chew. Meaning, do not do too many things at a time. Start something; finish it, and then move on to the next one. This way, you will avoid being overwhelmed and not finishing. It will also cause you to give it your all and produce nothing but the best.

"Write down, 10 different things that are bothering you right now, after reading this chapter."

_____

_____

_____

_____

_____

_____

_____

_____

_____

_____

_____

_____

_____

_____

_____

"Write down 10 things that you are grateful for after, reading this chapter."

_____

_____

_____

_____

_____

_____

_____

_____

_____

_____

_____

_____

_____

_____

_____

_____

_____

CHAPTER 6

KNOW WHO YOU ARE

People see you how you see yourself. If you think highly of yourself, others will think the same. You are all that, if you didn't know. I am here to tell you. One thing about me is my confidence is on one thousand. You can't tell me otherwise. Every day is a runway for me. I look my best even on my worst day. You have to look so good that the mirror comes to you to look in it. Look so good that you can kiss yourself! Know that you are all that in a bag of chips with a little bit of dip.

I love a verse Jada Kiss sang in a song. He said, "I'm not cocky; I'm confident. So, when you tell me I'm the best, it's a compliment." I'm the best thing since cooked food! I have what a lot of women lack, and that is confidence. Get some. Sometimes, we stay in a situation far too long because we don't know who we are. Once you tap into who you are, the rest is history. People cannot play you. People cannot mistreat you. People cannot talk to you anyhow because you know who you are. They have to put some respect on your name because you know who you are, and you are not going to tolerate any form of disrespect from anyone.

I remember people asking me why I always get my hair done, and I replied that I like to look good because first appearances leave lasting impressions. Nobody can ever say my hair is not done! These bonnets got to go. Understand that you look like a bum in the street with that on. Like no wonder people approach and talk to you in certain ways because of how you carry yourself. Carry yourself in such a way that whoever approaches you or wants to say something to you will think twice before saying it because you are not just anybody. You are the righteousness of God in Christ Jesus. They better recognize!

Showing your breast and butt cheeks does not mean you look good. You're naked, so, of course, people are going to look. You need to get a clue. The way you carry yourself determines the kind of men or women that approach you. Always keep that in mind. There is a time and season for everything. When you know who you are, you make it known even by how you carry and express yourself. Sometimes, we forget who we are, which is why we end up in the situation we find ourselves in, but once you realize that you are operating from a low place, you dust yourself off and take your rightful place.

Some people get out of one relationship into another. Stop that! It only hurts you more. You have to take time to work on yourself so as not to bleed on other people in the name of love. So many people change completely when they enter a relationship. Sometimes, the person you are in a relationship with will mold you into the person they want you to be, hence, losing yourself in the process. This is why, when you exit a relationship, it is good you take time out to work on yourself. Take control of yourself so that you are not this superficial person when you are ready to date again.

You have to strip off what they made you become and become who you are so that when you enter another relationship, that person gets the real you and not what the previous person made you turned you into.

Sometimes, you are so broken and destroyed when you exit a relationship that you don't feel like you could ever love or trust again. Understand that you can. There is someone out there to love everything about you, even what you hate about yourself. So, don't ever think you have to be or look like someone else to get or keep a man. You just have to be yourself, and whoever doesn't like you like that can get the stepping. They can go about their business because it is better to wait long than cry long. So, just wait for that person who will not be perfect but will be perfect for you.

"Write down, 10 different things that are bothering you right now, after reading this chapter."

_____

_____

_____

_____

_____

_____

_____

_____

_____

_____

_____

_____

_____

_____

_____

_____

_____

"Write down 10 things that you are grateful for after, reading this chapter."

_____

_____

_____

_____

_____

_____

_____

_____

_____

_____

_____

_____

_____

_____

_____

_____

_____

CHAPTER 7

STEP OUT AND FIND OUT

People will tell you; you can't do this; you can't do that. But I say you never know if you don't try it yourself. Do it afraid. Some people will tell you it's impossible because they cannot and were unable to do it. Don't let people limit you. God is in you, and you can do everything you put your mind to. So, don't let anyone stop you. Set your mind and keep it set. Have tunnel vision when it comes to your dreams and goals. Also, learn to keep your mouth shut and let it be known to you and God alone —no one else, until you know, for sure, that they have your best interest at heart.

I didn't know I could earn a master's degree. I just kept studying. My mother used to tell me all the time, "Lakisha, all you want to do is study." I just kept going. My mother never graduated from high school, and I knew that would never be me because she always pushed me to be better than her and achieve all she couldn't achieve. Some people undermined me and even stated I would be like my mother, but I disappointed them by achieving far above what their children could achieve! You never know what you can do until you try. Sometimes, you get scared as a human, but you shouldn't allow it to deter you from trying. Rather, you should do it afraid. I do it afraid all the time. I even do it shaking, and it's always worth it.

When I went to the dealership to get my vehicle, I was afraid, but I listened to my pastor and went. I had no money, just a car with a stubborn check engine light that would not come off. On August 28, 2021, I got up early and went to my mechanic, who had previously removed the check engine light. However, this time the check engine light will not come off. So, I said I just have to see if I can get money for this car. I went to a dealership in the Bronx with the intent of getting a used car, but God said no. God wanted me in a 2021 car, and that's what I eventually walked out of the dealership with. When I sat down with the financial guy, he said to me, "Let me get you in a 2021". I said, "Go ahead". That was nobody but God. This happened because I stepped out. I stepped out on faith, and I was able to get a 2021 model.

What is that thing you want to do or accomplish? What is stopping you? Who is stopping you? Step out now and find out. The answer you get could be yes, or not right now. But with God by your side, you will hear approved and congratulations. Sometimes, when fear kicks in, it is just to let you know that you should go for it as long as nothing will hurt you or your future. Time and time again, we let fear of the unknown stagnate us. We let it cripple us. Don't let it; it is a trick to perpetually keep you in your present state. Go for it; the sky is your limit.

I was introduced to stocks by a coworker, and it was a risk I had to take, but I did and made a few hundred dollars I didn't have before. Therefore, I started telling others about it, and they, too, made some money. But if I didn't step out, I wouldn't have made the money that came in so handy around last year's holiday season. So, don't always brush something off because it involves money or something new. Understand that change is good and needed. The same thing gets boring at times; hence also needs to be shaking up a little. Therefore, don't stay in a safe zone; it's not a good place to be. Step out of the box from time to time so that you can see and experience new things.

I was introduced to many restaurants and stores by my older brother, and till this day, I say, man, if he didn't take me to those stores or restaurants, I would still be eating and wearing the same things. Be open-minded when people are introducing you to something new. You never know, you might like it. Just because you have been eating the same thing or wearing the same label clothes does not mean you have to continue the same pattern. Things change, and seasons change, too, so don't be left behind out of ignorance.

"Write down, 10 different things that are bothering you right now, after reading this chapter."

_____

_____

_____

_____

_____

_____

_____

_____

_____

_____

_____

_____

_____

_____

_____

_____

"Write down 10 things that you are grateful for after, reading this chapter."

_____

_____

_____

_____

_____

_____

_____

_____

_____

_____

_____

_____

_____

_____

_____

CHAPTER 8

DON'T LOOK BACK

You cannot move forward if you keep looking back. You have to divorce history so that you can get to destiny. Stop looking and going back because there is nothing new there, only relics. Many doors open for us to move forward, but we get so comfortable in our present that we refuse to move. Yesterday is yesterday; it's not today; therefore, keep moving. People from our past often come into our lives just to see if we will let them back in. The only reason they come back is to see if we are still stupid. Some are just coming to use you, while others will come back to see if they can finish destroying you. Don't let them.

Looking back often seems like a good idea, but, in reality, it is not. It is a trap. In the Bible, we see Lot's wife turn into a pillar of salt after she looks back at the burning city of Sodom and Gomorrah. Genesis 19:26, "But his wife looked back from behind him, and she became a pillar of salt." This is why you have to be careful; the past will kill you. It will destroy you. Never look back because there is nothing good there. You never hear good stories about anyone who went back to their ex. It's awkward. They are your ex for a reason. If you thought it was that good, you would have stayed with them, but instead, you left them. There is nothing good there. This is why you remain in the same situation because you are your own enemy. You stop your blessing. Leave the past behind and reach forward to more excellent things God has in store for you.

At times, greater things lie right before you, but you can't see it because you keep looking back. The past has a way of making your future seem impossible. It also blurs your vision and makes it seem unreachable, but I am here to tell you that if you can only reach for it, you will understand why the enemy tried to keep you from it. You are not meant to be broke, busted, and disgusted. God has greater plans for you. So, if you find yourself in that situation, seek God and remain consistent, and you will see your life change for the better. You will be shocked by your progress and accomplishments. However, if you are going to experience a greater future, you have to press forward and don't look back.

What you experienced in your past was only preparing you for your future. That's why you cannot go back there. It had to happen the way it did. It had to hurt you the way it did. It was all to make you stronger. It was all to make you into the man and woman you are today. The lesson you learned will help you in this new season of your life. It will help you avoid the same pitfalls you once fell into. It will help you recognize the real from the fake. Nothing you go through is wasted.

I see now why the Bible says better is the end of a thing than the beginning of a thing. As human beings, we like what is comfortable, what we are used to. Therefore, we will remain in it. It is hard for us to get out of our comfort zones, which is why we make so many excuses and remain in it. You have to divorce yourself from the familiar because it will only keep you in bondage. Some people are aware it's time for you to go but refuse to sanction it because they have become comfortable using you, mistreating you, and treating you like a doormat. You didn't stop it, so they just continued. Why? Because you allowed them to. I heard Tony Gaskins say that you show people how to treat you by what you allow, stop, and reinforce.

I encourage you to work on yourself and think about a strategy to exit any situation you feel deep down is not right. Everyone is different, and some may be deep in it. In both cases, seek God, and He will show you what to do. Sometimes, walking away hurts. It's ok; nothing is easy. Just because it hurts doesn't mean you shouldn't do it. I had to walk away a lot of times when it hurt. But if you remain, they will continue to do what you allow them to do. A lot of people are users and manipulators. They will continue to do what they do because that's who they are and have been getting away with it for a long time. You just have to recognize it, move on, and never look back.

"Write down, 10 different things that are bothering you right now, after reading this chapter."

_____

_____

_____

_____

_____

_____

_____

_____

_____

_____

_____

_____

_____

_____

_____

_____

_____

_____

"Write down 10 things that you are grateful for after, reading this chapter."

_____

_____

_____

_____

_____

_____

_____

_____

_____

_____

_____

_____

_____

_____

_____

_____

_____

CHAPTER 9

EVERYTHING IS WORKING OUT FOR YOUR GOOD

You have to believe this, even the ugly things, the things that hurt, the things you cannot talk to anyone about but God, the thing that when you talk about, brings tears to your eyes. Understand that it has to work out this way. No storm lasts forever, even those things that look like you can never bounce back from. You will come out of it, but you must first believe that you can, even if it means taking baby steps, even if you have to crawl before you walk. Something is better than nothing. Baby steps are still progress.

People will come up with a lot of things to stop you. Understand that the weapons will form, but they will not prosper. God's Word is true, and it never comes back void. The enemy thinks that he is winning but even had to ask God for permission to mess with Job. So, know that no storm will last for eternity. It is a season, and when you come out of it, you will be surprised because you don't know what you can do or accomplish until you are placed in a position to just do it like Nike! Some of us won't move from a position unless a fire is lit underneath us. We will remain in a situation until it almost kills us before moving on. Others will remain due to a lack of adequate self-love or being too deep in it.

A lot of people try to stop me, especially on social media, with regard to business. My pages have been deleted and blocked from Instagram more than six times, but I just keep creating new pages. All the hate and jealousy just stirred me up to go harder. There are millions of people selling what I am selling, and they are bothering me—deleting my pages. This just shows me that I have a purpose, and the enemy does not want me to prosper, so they will use their people to stop me, but they are not God. The enemy does not know everything. They use people. That's it, and the Bible says that the enemy has their day to be stopped. So, never stop. I can't stop; I won't stop. The enemy will get tired of trying to mess with me because I will give them a run for their money, and you should do the same.

When God calls you, people can do whatever they want but not for as long as they want. The enemy has an expiration date. Know that. They cannot trouble you for too long. So, when you wake up in the morning, let the enemy be mad you're up because you are fighting back. Stay alert, so you know how to pray and slay that enemy every time they try to come for you. You know you are different when trials and tribulations come your way constantly. This is not something to fear because victory is already yours, and you will win every battle. It's a set fight. Why? Because God is on your side, and He will not cause your enemies to swallow you up. There is a set time for the enemy to be cut off!

When you come out of this storm, you will not look like what you have been through. You won't even smell like smoke. God will use the storm to take you to new levels and altitudes. When you come out, you will come out wiser and stronger. You are going to come out better than when you went in. The comeback is going to be so great than your setback. Those that once knew you would have to do a double-take because they will not be able to recognize the new you —the wiser you, the new you that doesn't settle for anything, the new you that accepts nothing but the best.

"Write down, 10 different things that are bothering you right now, after reading this chapter."

_____

_____

_____

_____

_____

_____

_____

_____

_____

_____

_____

_____

_____

_____

_____

_____

_____

"Write down 10 things that you are grateful for after, reading this chapter."

_____

_____

_____

_____

_____

_____

_____

_____

_____

_____

_____

_____

_____

_____

_____

_____

CHAPTER 10

IT WAS SET UP FOR YOU TO BE BLESSED

Somethings happen in your life to push you to the next level. When my mother passed away, I had no choice but to tap into that strong woman that my mother made me. My whole life revolved around my mom and Dad, and when my mother passed away, I felt empty. Yes, I had my dad with me, but it was different. Everything changed. I love my dad, but a mother's love is different. It was in this empty season of my life that I tapped into writing and entrepreneurship. Her demise was the worst thing to have ever happened to me, yet I birth three businesses and decided to write my book during this season. I am not sure if I would have started working on my first book or began my businesses if I hadn't had a push, if something didn't lead me to it. It was in losing that I gained.

After messing up my career as a correctional officer, God started opening doors after doors for me. I was able to meet people I no longer work with, yet we still communicate; I was able to pray for them while working there. It was all for a purpose. Everything you go through and will ever face in life will teach you something; try to discern them; it will always be needed for the next level of your life. Nothing is wasted. The tears, losses, stress, sleepless nights, and times you had to cry yourself to sleep all set you up for the wonderful person you are today. Everything you have ever gone through or will go through will all work together for your good and for your next level. Nothing you go through ever gets wasted. It will be used at some point in your life.

Seeds set you up for a blessing. When you are in need, sow a seed. I remember giving my last because I was expecting God to move and do something significant for me, and He did. I did a pop-up shop and wanted to make three or four times what I paid for the table, and I believed I would because I sowed that seed. God showed up and made the provision. It doesn't matter what you need from God; sow a seed to get it. Make it a habit to sow as many seeds as the harvest you want to reap because you never know when harvest time is. This is why it's good to have a lot of seeds in the ground.

Every time I give, I receive a blessing in return. It's like blessings run me down. I love to give. I am a giver. I take pride in giving. It is part of my DNA. This is why I have so much. I don't have to steal to get what I want. All I have to do is ask God for it, and if it aligns with His will, I will have it. If not, He will give me something better. We must learn to hold on to things lightly so the devil doesn't use them against us. Every time I give, I set myself self up for a blessing. It doesn't have to be a financial blessing; it could be good health, aversion of an accident, provision for my father, brother, sister-in-law, niece, or nephew because of the seeds I sow.

When you are going through it, it hurts and seems never-ending. But understand that you have to go through to get, TOO. Nothing comes easy. The blessings, the gifts, your anointing cost you something. This is why people need to stop being envious of you because they don't know what you had to go through to get what you have. It is not wise to envy someone else's things. What's for you will be for you. What has your name on it will not go to a different address. Many of us have not gotten what is due for us because we are busy hating, being envious, and jealous of someone else. Some of us even go as far as trying to stop someone's blessing, which is a major reason your blessings are being delayed because you are busy trying to stop someone else's blessing.

People try to stop my blessings all the time, but the more they try to, the more God blesses me in their face. It is dangerous trying to stop someone destined for greatness. You cannot stop someone who prays so much. Prayer is dangerous. Prayer will stop the assignment of the enemy for your life. When you know you are a good person and things are moving funny in your life, do me a favor and pray, and you will see the effects of your prayers. God will move on your behalf.

"Write down, 10 different things that are bothering you right now, after reading this chapter."

_____

_____

_____

_____

_____

_____

_____

_____

_____

_____

_____

_____

_____

_____

_____

_____

_____

_____

"Write down 10 things that you are grateful for after, reading this chapter."

_____

_____

_____

_____

_____

_____

_____

_____

_____

_____

_____

_____

_____

_____

_____

_____

CHAPTER 11

SHEDDING SEASON

D o you wonder, at times, why people are leaving your life or why the connection is no longer there? It is your shedding season. Some of them were into stuff you do not know about, but because you were connected to them, you get judged because of their fruits. This is why God had to remove them from your life. When you spend too much time with somebody, you end up being like them, doing what they do, and consequently, their bad habits end up on you. You see them compromising, and you end up doing things you would never have done if you weren't exposed to them. The fact that you watch them do it lures you into doing it, too. They will not judge you because they do the same thing as you. So, your standard doesn't have to be too high. This is why God has to separate you to raise your standards back up again.

There are people who you started off with that are nowhere to be found now. You don't even hang out or talk to them anymore. This could be one of two reasons, you have outgrown them, and the other is due to the friendship ending. It didn't have to be because of a fall out. However, there are other instances where there is a fall out. You may happen to disagree with them or be too honest with them, and they stop talking to you because of it. I had a friend whose boyfriend dogged her out, and she had obvious proof he was cheating on her, but because she saw her mother take her man back, time and time again after the disrespect, she, too, would do the same. One day, I asked her if she could stop acting like she was irrelevant without a man. She was upset, and after that, we stopped talking. I blocked her on everything. After I did, I realized a lot of negative things about her. If she called me because she wanted to talk about her man or how bad her day was going, or an incident at work, she would get upset if I didn't answer the phone. She was very clingy as a friend. She definitely had to go.

Some people come into your life for a reason and a season, while others come for a lifetime. I have friends I don't talk to every day, but I can always reach out to them whenever needed. Yet, when we talk, it is as if we just talked yesterday. Then you have your day ones; those are lifetime friends. You also have the ones that started with you but began to move funny along the way. Those kinds of friends now become associates. There are also friends you thought you would always have around you, yet they were jealous and envious of you the whole time. Those friends came around to teach you a lesson. You don't need a lot of friends; you only need a few good ones. I can count my good friend with one hand.

As you go up, people are going to fall off you. A lot of people are not on your level. Their mind is still in the past. They always talk about the past, and if you are not careful, they can take you back there. Having these types of friends around will keep you in the same place. These are friends with no vision for the future. They have not grown yet, and if you are not careful, they will keep you from prospering because they are stuck in the past. You need friends who will push you, friends who will encourage you to do big things. You need established friends who will let you into how they got there. You need friends that will help you. You don't need people in your circle who will stop your progress; you need those who push you to your destiny.

As the shedding takes place in your life, you might feel a little lonely because the people you started with will not be the ones you end up with. It is sad but good at the same time. Shedding season shows you the real from the fake. Shedding season is needed for you to grow into the person God has created you to be. In every season of your life, you are going to experience change. Don't be afraid of it because it is good. People change, and seasons change, so make sure you are up to date so you don't get left behind. The same thing gets boring at times.

Some of us are literarily in quicksand, but before we drown, God has to pull us out of it. He will remove people and push us into our place of purpose. He does this by removing people, opening doors, and allowing you to conquer new territory where you will meet new people that will help usher you into purpose. The prerequisite for the new is forgetting the old and reaching for the things before us. Don't be afraid of the new. Don't be intimidated or scared of new things. Expect and anticipate new doors, relationships, new moments, connections, and opportunities. You can not take old stuff with you as you move to new places. The old will not look good in the new. The old is too small to be transported into your new place. Reach for the new. Aggressively pursue the new. As you forget those things behind you, you will reach new levels. What you thought was your finish line was your starting point. Change your mindset so that you can reach your destination because greater things are in front of you, not behind. It is time to stop engaging your history so that you can marry your destiny. Change your number and marry destiny.

"Write down, 10 different things that are bothering you right now, after reading this chapter."

_____

_____

_____

_____

_____

_____

_____

_____

_____

_____

_____

_____

_____

_____

_____

_____

_____

"Write down 10 things that you are grateful for after, reading this chapter."

_____

_____

_____

_____

_____

_____

_____

_____

_____

_____

_____

_____

_____

_____

_____

_____

_____

_____

CHAPTER 12

THE BENEFITS OF WAITING

We are too impatient and don't want to wait for anything. Consequently, we end up in a mess we could have avoided if we had just waited. What you don't understand is that when you don't want to wait for anything, you end up with nothing. You end up with less than what God desires for you to have. Waiting preserves you. It keeps you from operating on impulse. It keeps you from the wrong things. Stop wrestling with the spirit of impatience. People may tell you, or even the enemy may remind you that time is running out, you are too old, you are still not married, you don't have a boyfriend, you don't have your own place, you have no children yet, etc., but I want you to know it's all a lie. Just wait on the Lord.

When it is your time, you will get all you need, and it will not burden you.

You will miss out on good things because you didn't wait. You will grab what you wanted but miss out on what you needed because you didn't wait. This is why we end up in relationships that are not good for us, relationships that break us down because we didn't wait and check the person out some more. Many of us rush into sleeping with someone we are yet to fully know then become confused and helpless when the person starts acting crazy. When you sleep with someone, emotions get involved, so your mind gets clouded. But if you had taken the time to get to know them, you would have seen their crazy self and avoided it. Now, you're entangled due to sexual relations with the person.

When you settle for what you want, you lose out on the best you could have had. We do better when we do it in God's way. When we operate on instant gratification, we end up with the bare minimum. We end up having to undo what we did before God would do what He wanted to do for us. In the Bible, we see that Isaac is the child of

79

promise and Ishmael is the child of flesh. Before Isaac could come, Abraham got impatient and ended up with Ismael. Abraham's wife, Sarah, was old and barren, so Abraham believed she could not conceive. Therefore, he impregnated his slave Hagar and Ishmael was the result. Then, later on, his wife had Isaac. If Abraham had waited, he would have just had what God promised him: Isaac.

When you wait, it renews you. When you settle, you get recycled things. You get old things. You cannot mix old with new. You want a new beginning, but being impatient will get you something that would ruin your new season. You cannot fix the old with the new. If you are believing God for new things and don't wait, you will get old things and wonder why they didn't work out. Wait for your good thing. When you mix old and new, it brings pressure. It will burst; it will not work out. Waiting is not a curse. Rather, it's an opportunity to prepare yourself for the season you are getting ready to experience. It gives you time to prepare yourself for what you want.

Have you ever seen people who get a position they are not ready for? Consequently, they are fired due to their inability to perform in that position. This is what being impatient does. If they had taken the time to train and prepare themselves, they would still have their position. If you give a baby a motorcycle, it will destroy the baby. This is the same thing. Whenever you get something prematurely, it will destroy you. It will cause you to have to start all over again.

Obtaining something prematurely will stress you out. It will be too much for you. It will cause confusion. It will not be clear. It will cause you to question too many things. This is how you know it's not the main thing. It brings a lot of problems and baggage with it. It causes you sleepless nights. So, take your time and don't rush because waiting will save your life.

Get into the habit of saying I don't want it a second before I am ready for it. This will stop you from receiving things that will harm you. Sometimes, we think we are ready for certain things when, in reality, we are not. Therefore, we often receive things prematurely and end up messing them up, and, in some instances, what we want ends up being a burden due to not being mature enough to receive it. It is like going to a dealership to get a brand-new car, knowing you earn minimum wage and would struggle to pay your car note and rent. You must wait for a while, use public transportation, start a business, get a better job, or do both. Then go back and get that car because you will be better off financially at this point.

Waiting will propel you forward. When you move too fast, you crash. You don't think about what you are doing. You make unnecessary mistakes. For example, when you are driving a vehicle and want to switch lanes, you just don't switch lanes; you wait, look in your mirror to make sure no other car is coming before moving to the next lane. Waiting will save your life. The world we live in operates on instant gratification. We want everything quickly, which is why we are so stressed and end up in unwanted messes. It is ok to take a step back and examine the situation. Take the time to decide before executing so that you are aware of what the outcome can be. Often, when we step out without taking time to examine the situation, we get entangled in things we would never have said yes to. Don't rush anything because the choices you make today will determine tomorrow's results. What you say yes to today will affect your tomorrow.

"Write down, 10 different things that are bothering you right now, after reading this chapter."

_____

_____

_____

_____

_____

_____

_____

_____

_____

_____

_____

_____

_____

_____

_____

_____

_____

"Write down 10 things that you are grateful for after, reading this chapter."

_____

_____

_____

_____

_____

_____

_____

_____

_____

_____

_____

_____

_____

_____

_____

_____

CHAPTER 13

EXPECT THE UNEXPECTED TO TAKE PLACE AT ANY GIVEN TIME

Everything can change at any given time. You will never remain in the same place for too long, especially if you're in a bad situation. There is a time and a season for everything. This is why you can rejoice and smile even in a bad situation. When unpleasant situations come your way, ask yourself what the situation wants to teach. There is always a lesson to be learned in every situation. I understand that unbearable situations may come your way and make you feel as though you will never get out of them, but I want you to know that trouble doesn't last and that everything you face will only make you stronger for the next level of your life. When you complain and murmur like the Israelites, you delay your blessing and prolong the duration of the situation. So, it's best to thank God in advance for what you expect Him to do.

Whenever you are going through the unexpected, expect a shift in your life at any given moment, but it won't happen unless you speak it. Often, you go through the unexpected, but there aren't many people around you to help you get out of the situation. I challenge you to encourage yourself. Speak life to yourself. Speak life to every area of your life that is not in alignment. Declare that everything will work together for your good, and every setback will be a setup for a greater comeback. Stay away from those who worsen your situation. Some people will help you stay low; those people need to be cut off and never let back into your life. You can come out of any situation by speaking your way out of it.

Know that God can do it for you at any given moment. Wake up every day with expectations, believing that this can be the day your life changes for the better. Your whole life can change physically, emotionally, and financially. What once troubled you can be history.

This is why you have to know that joy comes in the morning, and none of your troubles is a challenge to God. What we face is little compared to God. This is why we can all give God our burden, and He still feels no weight. Whenever you are faced with something, it is important that you cast your cares on God. Whatever is holding you back, stressing you out, and causing you sleepless nights, cast it on God; He wants all them all. He wants them as soon as you get them, not after trying and failing to deal with them. God wants your problems right away.

Don't allow anything to derail you. Often, the enemy sends people and things to take you from your path of purpose. When you know that you are called to do something, there will be many distractions to derail you from achieving it, distractions to take you out of destiny. May you recognize it and never let yourself be distracted from your purpose. Don't let anything or anybody distract you from your passion or what you want to do. May you never give in to the distraction that may come in your direction. May you recognize the distraction and let it propel you forward. May the distraction sent your way catapult you to your destiny.

If you are constantly stressing and worrying, you will never be able to live life abundantly. With all the uncertainties in the world, it is best to keep living it and trusting God to make all things work out for your good because that's what His Word says, and His Word never comes back to Him void. His Word also says in Jeremiah 29:11 (KJV), "For I know the thoughts that I think toward you, saith the Lord, thoughts of peace, and not of evil, to give you an expected end." This Scripture lets us know that God's plans for us are good, so we can trust Him and expect His plans for our life to surpass any problem that may come our way.

Oftentimes, we ask for things but doubt we would receive them. Try not to do that. When you ask God for something, wholly believe you have already received it but only waiting for its physical manifestation in your life. It is a process. Once you make the request, it goes from the supernatural to the natural. It doesn't matter what it is; just trust God because you will receive it, and in the event that you don't, you will still receive something that is best for you and aligns with God's will for your life. Many times we ask God for small things, but He does not give them to us because He has greater for us.

Be watchful. Things are taking off so fast. They are taking off like a rocket. Make sure you don't get left behind. Take doubt off your mind. What you are expecting from God will come in a way you never imagined. So, be watchful of your words, connection, and the seeds that you sow. That way, you don't delay your blessing by the negative words that come out of your mouth. 2022 will obey whatever you say, be it good or bad. At the end of the year, when you look back over the year 2022, it will look how you shaped it to be. It will look like the fruit of your words. It will look the way you spoke it into existence to be for you. In 2022, the soil is so ripe that it is ready to do what you speak for it to do for you. 2022 is the year of multiple doors and multiple increases. In 2022, expansions will come. Multiplication will come, but you have to be prepared for what is coming, be ready because what you are asking for will come when you least expect it. God will exceed your expectations.

This year, decree and declare that it will be your year of the unexpected. God is no respecter of persons. You don't have to be jealous or envious of someone else because what God does for one person, He can do for another person. Just ask God and wait for Him to give it to you. God is going to exceed your expectation in such a way that it is going to blow your mind. The unexpected will take place for you. 2022 will be the year of the unexpected. Be excited to be you because you are about to reach levels you never dreamed of. The only thing you have to do is expect the unexpected to happen at any given moment. So, be ready for the unexpected to happen for you at any given time.

"Write down, 10 different things that are bothering you right now, after reading this chapter."

_____

_____

_____

_____

_____

_____

_____

_____

_____

_____

_____

_____

_____

_____

_____

_____

_____

_____

LAKISHA WILLIAMS

"Write down 10 things that you are grateful for after, reading this chapter."

_____

_____

_____

_____

_____

_____

_____

_____

_____

_____

_____

_____

_____

_____

_____

_____

CHAPTER 14

SEEK PEACE

When you find yourself in a bad situation, the first thing you need to do is adjust your focus. You have to be careful of what you dwell on because whatever you are constantly thinking and worrying about will grow. This is why you have to shift your focus toward the positive direction. Your inner peace comes from focus. The flip side of that is confusion and chaos, which are often the results of a lack of focus. Life is going to happen, people will die, doors will close, and people will not like you. However, when you find yourself in those terrible situations, all you have to do is shift your focus to your good God.

When you have God's Word in your heart, your heart doesn't break easily, which is why the stuff that happens on the outside doesn't devastate me on the inside. It is because I have God hidden in my heart. God's Word keeps us from sinning and out of fear. Everything that has happened and will happen in your life is going to shape you, not break you. For this reason, you must adjust your focus. Learn to rejoice in all things and move your focus from what you lost to what you presently have. Change what you concentrate on.

If you are going to overcome anything, you have to refocus your mind, heart, and attention on good things. Don't focus on what you are going through; instead, focus on what God is bringing to you. Everything you will ever face has a purpose. So, never think why me. What you should be asking is why not me! The most tragic thing you can do with trauma and hurt is keep carrying it. Let it go. Don't be incarcerated by your past. Reach forward to those things that are ahead of you. When you are going through tough times, it is best to think of others and what you can do for them. That will turn your situation around when you take your mind off yourself and serve other people.

What you make happen for others, God will make happen for you. When you help others get through their moments, God will help you get through yours. God will do it when you decide to serve others instead of thinking about yourself. Even on the cross, Jesus was serving others. He lets a thief into the Kingdom while on the cross. Jesus served others while He was going through His season of suffering. So, don't get consumed in your season of suffering. Take your mind off of you so that you can get out of that place. While you are helping others, God is going to help you. God wants you to help others amid your trouble. When you do that, God will turn your situation around.

If you are going to find peace in a bad situation, you will have to give your pain to God through prayer. A lot of us act like we don't have pain. We just bleed on other people. We put on our public face while we have our private struggles. Give God your pain in exchange for healing and peace so you can have power in public. Some of us are going through unnecessary pain because we will not let God handle our cares. God's Word says in Philippians 4:6 (KJV), "Be careful for nothing; but in everything by prayer and supplication with thanksgiving let your requests be made known unto God." God wants to take your tragedy and give you back triumph. Don't go through anything alone. Give it to God. When prayer is a part of your life, you will never fall apart.

If you are going to make it through difficult times, you have to learn to pray and focus on something different. You will always get what you focus on. Focus on something good, and you will reap the benefits of something good. The Scripture says in Philippians 4:8 (KJV), "Finally, brethren, whatsoever things are true, whatsoever things are honest, whatsoever things are just, whatsoever things are pure, whatsoever things are lovely, whatsoever things are of good report; if there be any virtue, and if there be any praise, think on these things." This means that God wants us to focus on good things, not the things that will stress us out and make us lose sleep at night. A lot of things keep coming to your mind because you are talking about it. Let it go and stop anyone in your circle that continues to talk about a place where you no longer live or a season that you left behind. Don't dwell on circumstances. Dwell on good things!

If it cost you your peace, that is too expensive. Don't entertain it. It cost you too much. Don't entertain those determined to bring chaos and confusion into your life. Don't even answer them. Leave them unread. Do not answer them. In fact, block or delete every phone number to anyone that steals your peace or brings stress to your life. Keep a distance, no matter who they are. You don't want that kind of energy to rub off on you. Just like cheap, jealous, envious, and deceitful people, keep them away because you don't want that kind of energy rubbing off on you. Therefore, you must be willing to be alone in certain seasons. You cannot accomplish many things if you have certain people around you because they will distract you. They will take so much of your time that you won't have time for the important things. You will be busy taking care of their needs that when you turn around, your deadline or opportunity would have gone because you placed everyone before you. Help people but don't enable them. Some people will take advantage of you for as long as you let them. They will use you until you cut the cord. They will take your kindness for weakness. Recognize those people and don't allow them to drain you.

"Write down, 10 different things that are bothering you right now, after reading this chapter."

_____

_____

_____

_____

_____

_____

_____

_____

_____

_____

_____

_____

_____

_____

_____

"Write down 10 things that you are grateful for after, reading this chapter."

_____

_____

_____

_____

_____

_____

_____

_____

_____

_____

_____

_____

_____

_____

_____

_____

CHAPTER 15

DEAL WITH FIRE BUT DON'T LET IT GET CLOSE TO YOU

When you understand there is nothing new under the sun, you won't let the same situation get close to you again. The only one who can burn you is the one you grant access to you. You know the person is not good for you, yet you keep going back. You cannot be surprised when they do the same thing to you over and over again. It is who they are. You cannot expect something new to occur if you are still doing the same thing you used to do before. If you want new results, you have to do new things. When people show you who they are, believe them. Don't play the victim when you are a volunteer.

Whatever you willingly allow in your life that you know has the potential to hurt you is your fault because whatever you allow, you cannot complain about. Put relationships in proper perspective and put people in their proper place—some of those occupying the good seat in your life need to be expelled. Learn to discern. Know the people around you. Know the real from the fake. Learn to look people over. Know people's motives in your life so that you can know how to deal with them. Be wise enough to say, I've been burned already; that has happened to me already, so consequently, I will not entangle myself with them or that situation again.

Some people are not worth calling your friend. There are many people you have to feed with a long spoon. Sometimes, as a result of what has transpired, the relationship's parameters have to change. You might be friendly with them but not friends with them. There are people around you that are jealous, envious, and unhappy for you; they are poisonous. Keep your distance from them. Don't let them poison you. Abraham and Lot were family, but when Abraham discovered the friction with Lot, he went his own way. He wished him the best but kept his distance.

Stop letting your guard down to people that have injured, burned, and hurt you before. Some people did it out of wickedness. A lot of those who hit you was aiming at you. They meant to do it. It was their head and heart that wanted to do it. Don't let them have access to you again. Don't let an arsonist stay the night. They are not welcomed in your space. Keep them at a distance. The closer you allow a fire to you, the greater the degree of the burn. Watch people who won't give you space. Watch people who try to rush the relationship. Watch people who don't want to give you time to be in a relationship with them. Watch people who won't give you time and space to investigate who they are. Watch them. Satan will sneak up on you, so watch everybody that comes into your life.

You can't always give in to your nature. I am a loving person, but I know that I cannot be like that all the time. I have embraced people who have stabbed me in the back. So, I cannot give in to my human nature. I have to walk in the spirit. Check people's spirits out when they come around you. Some come to steal, kill and destroy you. So, you have to be very observant, conscious, and cognizant of the people around you. If you are not wise in your assessment and judge people by face value, you will be burned because everything that looks good is not good for you. Don't live your life disappointed and burned. Let people be proven in your life. Know the people around you. Pay attention to the warning before destruction comes. Learn to obey warning lights. Always be cautious of who you allow around you. Keep your eyes open.

Some people will swear with their life they have no issues with you and do not have a problem with you, yet in the spirit realm, they are placing your name on an evil altar, applying voodoo on you, and devising all sorts of means to harm you and bring you down. You must stay far from those kinds of people. They are wicked and don't even realize it. Some people are so wicked that they turn it up a notch when you stop or cut the cord. They even try harder to harm you. But you don't have to be afraid of anything anyone can or want to do to you because they need permission from God to do it, and even if they get it, it won't last forever; it's only for a little while. Every wicked person has their expiration date. They cannot do evil for too long ad get away with it.

Some will even stick around or remain close friends with someone you know just to get information about you. Therefore, you must be careful of who you talk to. Your may share mutual friends with the enemy without even knowing it. They may be playing both sides without your knowledge. They, too, must be cut off. When someone is playing both sides, cut them off because they may be the reason for your downfall. Some friends you least expect are jealous of you and would be the ones to sell your secrets out to your enemy. Sometimes, your enemy is closer than you think. Some of your enemies, who don't necessarily like each other, will even team up just to take you down. Why, because misery needs company.

"Write down, 10 different things that are bothering you right now, after reading this chapter."

_____

_____

_____

_____

_____

_____

_____

_____

_____

_____

_____

_____

_____

_____

"Write down 10 things that you are grateful for after, reading this chapter."

_____

_____

_____

_____

_____

_____

_____

_____

_____

_____

_____

_____

_____

_____

_____

SYNOPSIS

In this book, you will find the strategies I used to help me get through many difficult times in my life. I also, through experience, give insight on lessons and ways to live a prosperous life. In reading this book, I pray that it helps you open your eyes to ways to find the good in everything you may experience, be it good or bad. May God's favor be sufficient for you all the days of your life. God bless!

"Write down, 10 different things that are bothering you right now, after reading this chapter."

_____

_____

_____

_____

_____

_____

_____

_____

_____

_____

_____

_____

_____

_____

_____

_____

_____

"Write down 10 things that you are grateful for after, reading this chapter."

_____

_____

_____

_____

_____

_____

_____

_____

_____

_____

_____

_____

_____

_____

_____

_____

ABOUT THE AUTHOR

Lakisha Williams is a 35 years old trustworthy, family-oriented entrepreneur who loves the Lord and is quite full of life. She sees her life as an open book and loves to encourage people. Her personality is very youthful, which explains why children are so drawn to her. She loves people and enjoys helping in any way she can. As a lover of art, color and good sceneries attract her. She is very bold yet shy at times and enjoys traveling.

Aside from writing, she is also a beautician, and one of such businesses of hers can be viewed here: www.lashesbyfavor.com

"Write down, 10 different things that are bothering you right now, after reading this chapter."

_____

_____

_____

_____

_____

_____

_____

_____

_____

_____

_____

_____

_____

_____

_____

"Write down 10 things that you are grateful for after, reading this chapter."

_____

_____

_____

_____

_____

_____

_____

_____

_____

_____

_____

_____

_____

_____

_____

_____

Made in the USA
Middletown, DE
12 February 2022

60989183R00066